AF480846

GREAT Women

JOURNAL

Fidel M. Donaldson

"The Lord gives the command; The women who proclaim the good tidings are a great host"

New American Standard Bible

Great Women Journal

ISBN 979-8-89074-154-7

LCCN 2017935889

Cover Design & Layout by D'Edge Media / dedgemedia.com
Printed in the United States of America

TRIUMPH OVER TRAGEDY

Great Women Journal

Date:

Great Women Journal

Date:

Great Women Journal

Date:

Great Women Journal

Date:

Great Women Journal

Date:

Great Women Journal

Date:

Great Women Journal

Date:

Great Women Journal

Date:

Great Women Journal

Date:

Great Women Journal

Great Women Journal

Date:

Great Women Journal

Date:

Great Women Journal

Date:

Great Women Journal

Date:

Great Women Journal

Date:

PIONEERS, TRAILBLAZERS & TRENDSETTERS

- *Paradigm Shifters*
- *Leadership To Leader-Shift*
- *God's Woman On The Inside*

Great Women Journal

Date:

Great Women Journal

Date:

Great Women Journal

Date:

Great Women Journal

Date:

Great Women Journal

Date:

Great Women Journal

Date:

Great Women Journal

Great Women Journal

Date:

Great Women Journal

Date:

Great Women Journal

Date:

Date:

Great Women Journal

Date:

Great Women Journal

Date:

Great Women Journal

Date:

POWER, PASSION & PURPOSE IN PRAYER

Great Women Journal

Date:

Great Women Journal

Date:

Great Women Journal

Date:

Great Women Journal

Date:

Great Women Journal

Date:

Great Women Journal

Date:

Great Women Journal

Date:

Great Women Journal

Date:

Great Women Journal

Date:

THE PROPHETIC ENCOUNTER

- *Last Shall Be First*
- *The Chazaq Anointing*
- *The Prophetic Awakening*

Great Women Journal

Date:

Great Women Journal

Date:

Great Women Journal

Date:

Great Women Journal

Date:

Great Women Journal

Date:

Great Women Journal

Great Women Journal

Date:

Great Women Journal

Date:

Great Women Journal

Date:

Great Women Journal

Date:

Great Women Journal

Date:

Great Women Journal

Date:

Great Women Journal

Great Women Journal

Date:

Precious Jewels

DIAMONDS
IN THE ROUGH

- *Positioned For Divine Purpose*
- *Blessed And Highly Favored*
- *Don't Need The Spotlight*

Great Women Journal

Date:

Great Women Journal

Date:

Great Women Journal

Date:

Great Women Journal

Date:

Great Women Journal

Date:

Great Women Journal

Date:

Great Women Journal

Date:

Great Women Journal

Date:

Great Women Journal

Date:

Great Women Journal

Date:

TRUE WORSHIP

Great Women Journal

Date:

Date:

Great Women Journal

Date:

Great Women Journal

Date:

Great Women Journal

Date:

Great Women Journal

Date:

Great Women Journal

Date:

Great Women Journal

Great Women Journal

Date:

Section Seven

When The
STORM BREAKS

• Brilliant Strategies
• From The Whorehouse To The Lord's
• House Hidden Figures-Dear Men

Great Women Journal

Great Women Journal

Date:

Great Women Journal

Great Women Journal

Date:

Great Women Journal

Date:

Great Women Journal

Date:

Great Women Journal

Great Women Journal

Date:

Date: